Dinner

Desserts & Sweet Treats 99

Condiments 111

Your 7 Day Meal Planner 117

JANE WRIGHT

the
sirtfood
diet recipe book

Over 100 Delicious Calorie-Counted Recipes
to Burn Fat, Lose Weight and Get Leaner!

First published in 2015 by Erin Rose Publishing

Text and illustration copyright © 2015 Erin Rose Publishing

Design: Julie Anson

ISBN: 978-0-9933204-4-6

A CIP record for this book is available from the British Library.

DISCLAIMER: This book is for informational purposes only and not intended as a substitute for the medical advice, diagnosis or treatment of a physician or qualified healthcare provider. The reader should consult a physician before undertaking a new health care regime and in all matters relating to his/her health, and particularly with respect to any symptoms that may require diagnosis or medical attention.

While every care has been taken in compiling the recipes for this book we cannot accept responsibility for any problems which arise as a result of preparing one of the recipes. The author and publisher disclaim responsibility for any adverse effects that may arise from the use or application of the recipes in this book. Some of the recipes in this book include nuts and eggs. If you have an egg or nut allergy it's important to avoid these.

CONTENTS

Recipes
Smoothies

Breakfast 37

Lunch 47

Introduction

The SIRTfood Diet is a revolutionary new approach to eating that combines incorporating much more of certain sirtuin-activating 'wonder foods' into your diet, together with some elements of IF ' Intermittent Fasting' to activate your 'weight loss' gene, restore cell function and renewal and increase valuable body muscle mass. So you not only lose weight and gain lean muscle, which in turn increases your metabolism, but you can actually improve your body's cell function and your overall health and wellbeing too!

'Sirtuins' are a class of proteins within mammals, including humans, that control cellular processes in the body such as inflammation, metabolism, ageing and cell function. The human body has seven sirtuins, each with its own functions, but it is the recent discovery of the magical ' SIRT1' gene that promises to revolutionise our health and our approach to dieting and eating in the future.

The 'SIRT1' gene, aka the 'Skinny Gene', inhibits the storage of fat and also increases fat metabolism and so it can be incredibly effective for weight loss. SIRT1 has already been the focus of the recently successful '5:2 Diet', with studies showing that calorie restriction in the form of Intermittent Fasting can actually help activate our SIRT1 gene. By switching on this gene via fasting, the body can begin to repair any damaged cells and those on the diet have reported significant improvements in a wide variety of health issues and ailments. As a result of reducing their calorie intake significantly 2 days a week, plus the metabolism boosting effects, they also report excellent weight loss benefits too.

The new 'SIRTfood' diet takes this knowledge a step further and recent research into foods has shown that a certain key list of foods – now known as 'SIRT foods' - when eaten in suitable quantities can also have the effect of activating that magic SIRT1 gene.

While 'superfoods' and their benefits have been widely known and used in diet and nutrition approaches for some time now, the discovery of the SIRT1 gene combined with recent research into these specific sirtuin-activating 'SIRT foods' looks set to be a game changer!

Until now some of these foods were known for being terrific antioxidants by preventing free radical damage but now it seems these super foods have an even more important and profound benefit to our health.

While the already obviously healthy foods like leafy green veg, apples and citrus fruits make the SIRTfoods list – the great news is that the list also includes dark chocolate and red wine!

While many diets encourage the eating or inclusion of certain foods to encourage weight loss, this tends to be purely due to the low calorific content of these foods and usually has no bearing on the actual nutritional quality or benefits to your health.

The SIRTfood diet is all about boosting your intake of nutritious 'skinny gene' activating foods which is welcome news to anyone who has been on a restrictive diet, because this is an 'inclusive' way of eating which boosts your intake of fresh and revitalising foods. By eating specific foods that can activate your metabolism-boosting SIRT1 gene, you can utilise your diet to help burn off excess fat and increase muscle mass in the body.

The diet industry is about to undergo its most radical change yet and pharmaceutical companies have already tried and failed to harness, process and synthesize the benefits of these SIRT foods. However, Mother Nature provided these fabulous foods in natural abundance in a form which our bodies can assimilate naturally, without the need for tablets, concentrations or chemical intervention and that's the beauty of the SIRTfood diet – it's natural!

This SIRTfood Diet Recipe Book is the perfect companion book to the more detailed research-heavy SIRT Diet books out there and is perfect for anyone embarking on the SIRTfood diet and in need of food inspiration!

With tons of healthy and delicious recipes high in SIRT1-activating foods, plus a great selection of super SIRT1-activating smoothies to assist with low calorie days, this book will ensure that your days on the SIRTfood diet are super and delicious!

SIRT 1-
'The Skinny Gene' And How It Works

The SIRTfood diet is more than just a weight loss diet, it is also a way of improving your health, as not only does it help people shed unwanted pounds and most importantly keep them off, it slows down the ageing process and helps reduce inflammation and for this we have to credit the activation of the 'skinny' gene or 'SIRT1', its proper name.

It basically works like this. There are 7 SIRT genes in total but SIRT1 is the 'skinny gene'. The skinny gene is activated by intermittent calorie restriction and by SIRT foods which contain resveratrol. The benefits of 'skinny gene' SIRT1 are that it protects cells to improve survival in times of stress and it seems that restricting calories and reduced consumption of food causes the gene to activate to protect the body from scarce food supply. SIRT1 steps in to protect cells from dying off and preventing free radical damage by activating higher energy production of the cells. This higher energy production by the cells is fuelled by stored fat, as the metabolism increases, which leads to...you guessed it, weight loss!

It may seem deceptive that we are creating a situation in our body where it thinks there is a risk, but it's actually how our bodies used to function – before the introduction of junk foods and too much food in general – way back when we had fewer meals per day and ate more fresh produce grown more locally. Let's remember the calorie restriction in this diet is not extreme or dangerous. This is not simulated starvation. We are actually restoring out bodies to a time when our lifestyles were healthier and obesity, diabetes, heart disease and inflammatory diseases were less common than they are today.

So we can see how weight loss occurs when the body's metabolism is cranked up by the SIRT1 gene but let's look at the anti-ageing and anti-inflammatory aspect. When the SIRT1 gene kicks in to protect the cells from oxidative stress from free radicals (many of the SIRT foods are already well known for being high in antioxidants) it results in fewer of the free radical cells which cause inflammation and accelerated ageing.

Oxidative stress in the body is implicated in impaired immune function, wrinkles, age spots and saggy skin and diseases such as heart disease, Alzheimer's, cancer etc. It occurs when the body has more free radicals (oxidants) than it can neutralise and detoxify with antioxidants. It's a clever balancing act to protect the body from toxicity. When oxidative stress is reduced, healing can take place.

So you can see this isn't just a diet about weight loss, it's a way of eating to safeguard your health, now and in the future. By activating the SIRT1 gene, with SIRT foods and calorie restriction, not only can you get down to a healthy weight that is right for you but you can improve your health at the same time. And the really good news is, you can do this while including chocolate and red wine in your diet!

The Benefits Of The SIRTfood Diet?

The SIRTfood diet is a healthy way of introducing sirtuin-activating super foods into your diet and it is suitable for most people. There are seven sirtuins (SIRT1 – SIRT7) which are a type of protein which regulate inflammation, stress resistance, metabolism and affect longevity due to selective regulation of cell death. These sirtuins provide protection for the body particularly when under stress and can improve lifespan by protecting from diseases.

The Benefits of SIRTfoods:
- Improved resistance to stress
- Improve overall health and increase longevity
- Decreased signs of ageing
- Improved metabolism
- Healthy weight loss
- Anti-inflammatory benefits

Ways To Reduce Oxidative Stress

- Don't overeat and especially over consume sugars and starchy carbohydrates.

- Stop smoking (or reduce it at least).

- Reduce pollutants you inhale. While this may not be possible in your public environment, you can do this at home by reducing chemicals from air fresheners and cleaning products.

- There are supplements available which contains antioxidants and resveratrol but the best way to get your nutrients are through fresh, whole and unprocessed foods.

What Are the SIRT Foods?

This seems such a humble little line up compared to their amazing capabilities and most of us are already familiar with these staple foods. We already know that some of these foods are super healthy and the general benefits are listed below, but we are really interested in them for their ability to switch on the sirtuin genes to burn fat, improve muscle tone and promote good health.

Introducing the SIRT foods:

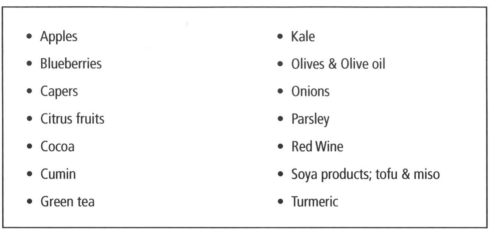

- Apples
- Blueberries
- Capers
- Citrus fruits
- Cocoa
- Cumin
- Green tea

- Kale
- Olives & Olive oil
- Onions
- Parsley
- Red Wine
- Soya products; tofu & miso
- Turmeric

For years we've known about the health benefits that have led some of these foods to commonly be called 'superfoods' but here is a reminder and you can also see how this ties in with sirtuins too!

Apples

Apples are known to be packed with vitamin C and pectin. Cooked apples were also a traditional remedy for constipation. They are a valuable source of fibre and have been linked to weight loss.

Blueberries

These 'wonder berries' are packed with nutrients such as potassium, vitamin K, antioxidants, folate and fibre which is known to reduce cholesterol.

Capers

This less well known food is actually a pea-sized flower bud which contains phytonutrients, antioxidants, iron, calcium, vitamins and they are known to benefit the skin and protect against free radical damage. They also contain quercetin which is antibacterial, anti-carcinogenic and anti-inflammatory. They were an ancient treatment for rheumatic pains probably due to their anti-inflammatory abilities.

Citrus Fruits
Oranges, grapefruits, lemons and limes all contain vitamin C and provide antioxidants and dietary fibre. They boost immunity, prevent constipation and they are also valuable sources of pectin, which can help reduce cholesterol.

Cocoa
Cocoa improves blood vessel health and benefits blood pressure and cholesterol. It contains flavonoids which are antioxidants that are also found in fruit and vegetables. It improves cholesterol. It is the sugar that's been added that can be a problem, so always go for good quality dark chocolate that has at least 70% cocoa, or cocoa nibs.

Green Tea
Green tea is packed with nutrients and antioxidants which lower the risk of cancer and it has been shown to improve weight loss and benefit brain function. You can replace your usual tea or coffee with green tea plus you won't need to add milk or sugar which would otherwise add to your calorie intake.

Kale
Contains iron, calcium, folate, beta carotene and Vitamin C - which are antioxidants known to offer protection against cancer.

Olives & Olive Oil
Olives are a great source of Vitamin E and antioxidants. Helps balance good and bad cholesterol levels. Contains monounsaturated fatty acids which help lower the risk of heart disease.

Onions
This common and often underused vegetable contains chromium which helps to regulate blood sugar. They were traditionally used as a 'cure all' to fight

infections and reduce inflammation.

Parsley
A real power herb which contains vitamins which benefit the immune system, bones and help rid the body of excess fluid. It also contains flavonoid antioxidants.

Red Wine
We know that red wine in moderation can have benefits because it contains resveratrol which helps reduce cholesterol levels and it also contains antioxidants.

Soya Products; Tofu & Miso
Soya can prevent the absorption of cholesterol and can lower the risk of breast cancer and osteoporosis.

Turmeric & Cumin
Both these delicious spices contain curcumin which is a strong anti-inflammatory compound and a powerful antioxidant.

Calorie Contents of SIRT Foods

The purpose of this section is to give you an indication of the calorie contents of the individual foods to let you see how much of them you can consume and still be aware of your calorie intake. For instance, if you are snacking or replacing a meal with helpings of fruit, you can weigh them and see how many calories you are consuming.

Apples	52 calories per 100g
Blueberries	57 calories per 100g
Capers	23 calories per 100g
Citrus Fruits; Oranges	47 calories per 100g
Grapefruits	33 calories per 100g
Lemons	24 calories per fruit
Limes	20 calories per fruit
Cocoa powder (100%)	12 calories per tablespoon
Green tea	0 calories per teabag
Kale	49 calories per 100g
Olive oil	40 calories per teaspoon
Onions	40 calories per 100g
Parsley	36 calories per 100g
Red Wine	125 calories per 5fl oz serving
Tofu (soya)	76 calories per 100 grams
Turmeric	8 calories per teaspoon

Getting Started

You can start incorporating SIRT foods into your diet straight away. Make sure you familiarise yourself with the list of foods and source out good quality ingredients.

The SIRTfood diet can be approached in 2 ways:

1. Simply by including these powerful foods into your daily diet and maximising your nutrient intake from these plants.

OR

2. By introducing these delicious foods into your diet in abundance and using Intermittent Fasting to restrict your calorie intake on some days to maximise weight loss.

Decide on whether you wish to restrict your calorie intake to make the most of your weight loss.

If you decide on calorie restriction as well as incorporating SIRT foods, your aim is to stay within the following maximum daily calorie intake:

---

3 days – 1000 calories per day

4 days – 1500 calories per day

Pack in the activating SIRT foods into all meals. Ideally, at least two meals a day should consist of high sirtuin-activating smoothies – perhaps for breakfast and lunch - as these are an easy way of piling in high amounts of the SIRT foods whilst staying within your calorie limit, then follow these with a balanced evening meal.

Exercise

As with any weight-loss plan, regular moderate exercise is key to boost your energy and maximise weight-loss. Take **MODERATE** exercise. Too much exercise can increase oxidative stress, but as a guide between 30 and 60 minutes a day is optimal. If you currently do very little exercise you can start with walking or swimming and increase it if necessary.

The Maintenance Plan

You can stick to your SIRTfood diet for a week or a month or as long as you like – the real reward is noticing the positive health benefits and maintaining a healthy weight. Eating abundant naturally healthy foods will always be good for you. You don't have to restrict calories, however overeating will of course eventually lead to weight gain.

SIRT foods are naturally packed with nutrients and introducing and keeping these tasty foods in your diet can be your new normal. Losing unwanted weight and enjoying better vitality will give you the encouragement to keep going. Once you've discovered which recipes work well for you will find it so much easier.

The Wine and Chocolate Diet?

Recent press on the SIRTfood diet has jumped on the 'eat lots of chocolate and drink red wine and still lose weight' angle – but it's pretty obvious to most of us that overindulging in either would in fact have the opposite effect! So of course, it's all about moderation – don't go crazy and over indulge in bars of chocolate, especially low quality, high sugar chocolate. It's the cocoa in chocolate which is good for you – sugar is NOT. If you've found a great dark chocolate, over 70% cocoa content (the higher the cocoa content, the lower the sugar) that is great! Stick with it and a square or two of chocolate after a meal as a treat is well deserved.

As for red wine, stay within the daily recommended alcohol limits. The current guidelines for men are 3-4 units of alcohol a day and 2-3 units a day for women. To clarify, one unit of red wine is about 85mls (approx 3fl oz) but it varies according to the alcohol content. Plus all those calories still have to be factored in – do you really want to drink your calorie allowance?

So while you can enjoy chocolate or wine in moderation, a whole bar or a whole bottle is sadly not part of the plan!

Cooking On The SIRTfood Diet

Most of our recipes will fit easily into a busy lifestyle and they are simple to follow. With any diet, the greatest challenge comes from feeling deprived by restrictions to what you can eat. However, on the SIRTfood diet no food is out of bounds, just continue to make healthy choices and you can't go far wrong. If you experiment with the recipes you can substitute some of the ingredients to create your own favourite dishes. They don't need to be elaborate, just simple and tasty.

It's a good idea to invest in a good blender to make the smoothies. The Nutribullet is excellent for this purpose. Smoothies are a great way of combining low-calorie ingredients in a fast and nutritious meal which means you can really load up the nutrients without having to cook.

Start by stocking up on your store cupboard essentials – like swapping whatever vegetable oil you use to extra-virgin olive oil – or replace readymade curry sauce jars by making your own spice mixes, ensuring you add turmeric and cumin. For those who would usually buy frozen peas or a head of broccoli in their weekly shop, you can add in a bag or two of kale and replace the vegetable portion of a meal with that instead. You can swap your usual tea or coffee for green tea. By making simple changes your eating habits will change and your health will improve.

We hope you enjoy the recipes. Wishing you great health!

Recipes

SMOOTHIES

Super SIRT Food Smoothie

Ingredients

75g (3oz) blueberries
50g (2oz) kale
1 medium apple, cored
1 medium orange
300mls (½ pint) green tea (made the night before and cooled)
Juice of ½ lemon
Ice cubes or crushed ice

SERVES 1

173 calories per serving

Method

Place all of the ingredients into a blender and blitz until smooth. You can add extra water or cool green tea if you need to thin the smoothie.

Clementine & Banana Smoothie

Ingredients

4 freshly squeezed juice of
4 clementine oranges
1 banana
1 apple
1 avocado, de-stoned and peele

SERVES
1

254
calories
per
serving

Method

Place all of the ingredients into a food processor with enough water to cover them and process until smooth.

Kale & Grapefruit Smoothie

Ingredients

1 carrot
1 grapefruit, peeled
1 apple, cored
25g (1oz) kale

SERVES
1

132
calories
per
serving

Method

Place the ingredients into a blender with sufficient water to cover them and blitz until smooth.

Creamy Citrus Blend

Ingredients

1 ripe avocado, de-stone and peeled
1 orange, peeled
1 apple, cored
Juice of 1 lime

**SERVES
1**

**393
calories
per
serving**

Method

Place all the ingredients into a blender with enough water to cover and blitz until smooth.

Apple & Kale Smoothie

Ingredients

1 apple, cored
1 orange, peeled
25g (1oz) kale
1 tablespoon sunflower seeds

**SERVES
4**

**209
calories
per
serving**

Method

Place all the ingredients into a blender and add around a cup of water. Blitz until smooth. You can add a little extra water if it's too thick.

Cherry & Blueberry Smoothie

Ingredients
- 100g (3½ oz) blueberries
- 75g (3oz) frozen pitted cherries
- 1 tablespoon plain Greek yogurt
- 200mls (7fl oz) unsweetened soya milk

SERVES 1

188 calories per serving

Method
Place all of the ingredients into a blender and process until smooth.

Coconut & Chocolate Smoothie

Ingredients
- 60mls (2fl oz) coconut milk
- 60mls (2fl oz) unsweetened soya milk
- 75g (3oz) pineapple
- 75g (3oz) kale
- 1 tablespoon 100% cocoa powder or cacao nibs
- A few ice cubes

SERVES 1

204 calories per serving

Method
Place all of the ingredients into a blender and process until smooth. You can add the ice cubes after blending if preferred.

Apple & Almond Smoothie

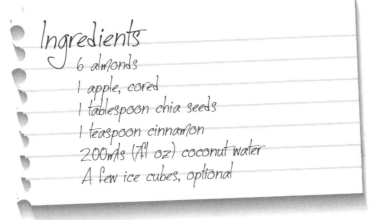

Ingredients
- 6 almonds
- 1 apple, cored
- 1 tablespoon chia seeds
- 1 teaspoon cinnamon
- 200mls (7fl oz) coconut water
- A few ice cubes, optional

SERVES 1

225 calories per serving

Method

Place all of the ingredients into a blender and process until smooth. If your blender isn't suitable for ice cubes you can add a few ice cubes after mixing.

Banana, Walnut & Cinnamon Smoothie

Ingredients
- 1 apple
- 1 banana
- 6 walnuts
- 1/4 teaspoon cinnamon

SERVES 4

270 calories per serving

Method

Place all of the ingredients into a blender with a little water to cover them and process until smooth and creamy. You can add a few chopped walnuts to the top if you wish with an extra sprinkling of cinnamon.

Kale & Papaya Smoothie

Ingredients
75g (3oz) kale
½ papaya, seeds and skin removed
1 apple
Juice of ½ lemon

SERVES 1

160 calories per serving

Method

Place all of the ingredients into a blender with enough water to cover then and process until smooth.

Chocolate & Banana Smoothie

Ingredients
1 banana
100mls soya milk
2 tablespoons 100% cocoa powder or cacao nibs
1 tablespoon chia seeds

SERVES 1

204 calories per serving

Method

Place all the ingredients into a food processor and mix until smooth and creamy.

Cherry Chocolate Smoothie

Ingredients

- 10 cherries, stones removed
- 5 strawberries
- 50g (2oz) blueberries
- 1 tablespoon 100% cocoa powder or cacao nibs
- ½ avocado de-stoned & peeled
- 200mls (7fl oz) unsweetened soya milk

SERVES 1

290 calories per serving

Method

Place the ingredients into a blender and process until smooth and creamy.

Tropical Green Smoothie

Ingredients

- ½ avocado, de-stoned, peeled and roughly chopped
- 25g (1oz) spinach
- 50g (2oz) kale
- 50g (2oz) fresh pineapple, chopped
- 200mls (7fl oz) coconut water

SERVES 1

219 calories per serving

Method

Put the avocado, spinach, kale and pineapple into the blender, top up with coconut water, then blitz until smooth.

Chocolate & Peach Smoothie

Ingredients

1 peach, stone removed
75g (3oz) fresh pineapple, chopped
50g (2oz) kale
50g (2oz) blueberries
1 tablespoon 100% cocoa powder or cacao nibs
200mls (7fl oz) unsweetened soya milk

SERVES
1

196
calories
per
serving

Method

Place all of the ingredients into a blender and process until smooth.

Pomegranate & Blueberry Smoothie

Ingredients

75g (3oz) blueberries
50g (2oz) kale
120mls unsweetened pomegranate juice
1 teaspoon chia seeds

SERVES
1

155
calories
per
serving

Method

Place all the ingredients into a blender with enough water to cover them and blitz until smooth.

Grape, Avocado & Kale Smoothie

Ingredients

75g (3oz) green grapes
75g (3oz) kale
1 avocado, de-stoned and peeled
Juice of 1 lime

SERVES 1

352 calories per serving

Method

Place all of the ingredients into a blender with enough water to cover them and process until smooth.

Creamy Chilled Strawberry Smoothie

Ingredients

50g (2oz) frozen blueberries
50g (2oz) frozen strawberries
125g (4oz) plain unflavoured yogurt
100mls (3 ½ oz) unsweetened soya milk

SERVES 1

162 calories per serving

Method

Whizz the berries, yogurt and soya milk together in a blender and process until smooth.

Mango & Kale Smoothie

Ingredients

25g (1oz) fresh kale,
150g (5oz) mango flesh
1/2 avocado, de-stoned and peeled
200mls (7fl oz) unsweetened soya milk

SERVES 1

285 calories per serving

Method

Place all of the ingredients into a blender and process until smooth. Enjoy.

Carrot & Orange Smoothie

Ingredients

150g (5oz) blueberries
1 medium carrot, peeled
1 apple, cored
1 large orange, peeled
Juice of 1 lime

SERVES 1

217 calories per serving

Method

Place all of the ingredients into a blender with enough water to cover them and blitz until smooth.

35

Forest Fruits Smoothie

Ingredients

125g (4oz) frozen mixed frozen fruits
125g plain unflavoured yogurt
1 banana
1 apple
100mls (3½ fl oz) unsweetened soya milk

SERVES
1

288
calories
per
serving

Method

Place all of the ingredients into a food processor and blitz until smooth and creamy.

BREAKFAST

Chilled Blueberry Porridge

Ingredients

100g (4oz) blueberries
50g (2oz) rolled oats
200mls (7fl oz) unsweetened soya milk
2 teaspoons chia seeds
100ml (3½ fl oz) water

SERVES 1

321 calories per serving

Method

Place the blueberries, oats, soya milk and water into a blender and process until smooth. Stir in the chia seeds and mix well. Chill before serving. This is a great breakfast for summer mornings which can be prepared the night before.

Apple & Cashew Nut Crunch

Ingredients

100g (3½ oz) plain Greek yogurt
1 apple, peeled, cored and finely chopped
10 unsalted cashew nuts, chopped

SERVES 1

241 calories per serving

Method

Stir half of the chopped apple into the yogurt. Using a glass, place a layer of yogurt with a sprinkling of apple and a sprinkling of cashews, followed by another layer of the same until you reach the top of the glass. Garnish with cashew pieces.

Feta & Kale Mini Omelettes

Ingredients

4 large eggs
50g (2oz) feta cheese, crumbled
75g (3oz) kale leaves, finely chopped
1 tablespoon parsley

SERVES 4

113 calories per serving

Method

Place the kale in a steamer and cook for about 5 minutes until tender. In a bowl, whisk the eggs together then add the feta cheese and parsley. Stir the kale into the mixture. Lightly grease a 4 portion muffin tin. Pour in the egg and kale mixture. Bake in the oven at 180C/350F for around 20 minutes until the eggs are set. Enjoy. These can be enjoyed warm or cold.

Granola

Ingredients

225g (8oz) oats
2 tablespoons sesame seeds
2 tablespoons sunflower seeds
50g (2oz) flaked almonds
50g (2oz) dried apple, chopped
50g (2oz) dried blueberries
2 teaspoons honey
2 tablespoons olive oil
25mls (1fl oz) fresh orange juice

SERVES 10

211 calories per serving

Method

Place the oats, sesame seeds, sunflower seeds, almonds and dried fruit into a bowl and mix well. In a separate box combine the honey, olive oil and orange juice then pour it into the oats mixture and combine. Spread out the mixture on a baking sheet. Transfer it to the oven and bake at 160C/325F for 35 minutes. Allow it to cool then store it in an airtight container until ready to use.

Blueberry Compote & Cinnamon Yogurt

Ingredients

200g (7oz) blueberries
200g (7oz) plain Greek yogurt
1 star anise
½ teaspoon cinnamon
100mls (3½ oz) water

SERVES 2

178 calories per serving

Method

Place the blueberries and star anise into a saucepan, add the water and bring to the boil. Reduce the heat and simmer for 10 minutes or until the blueberries have burst open. Discard the star anise, remove the saucepan from the heat and set aside to cool. Stir the cinnamon into the yogurt then serve it into bowls. Spoon the blueberry compote over the top and eat immediately.

Mediterranean Frittata

Ingredients

100g (3½ oz) cheese, grated (shredded)
8 black olives
6 large eggs
8 cherry tomatoes, halved
4 spring onions (scallions), chopped
1 small courgette (zucchini), sliced
2 tablespoons fresh basil
2 tablespoons fresh parsley
1 tablespoon olive oil
Sea salt
Freshly ground black pepper

SERVES 4

267 calories per serving

Method

Cut the olives into half, removing all stones. Whisk the eggs in a bowl and season with salt and pepper. Add in the spring onions (scallions), courgette (zucchini), basil and parsley. Heat the oil in a small frying pan and pour in the egg mixture. Add in the tomatoes and olives, cut side up. Sprinkle with cheese. Cook until the mixture completely sets. Place the frittata under a hot grill for 2 minutes then remove it from the pan. Cut into slices and serve.

Fried Cinnamon Apple & Halloumi

Ingredients

50g (2 oz) halloumi cheese, sliced
1 apple, peeled, cored and sliced
½ tablespoon olive oil
Sprinkling of cinnamon

SERVES
1

246
calories
per
serving

Method

Heat the olive oil in a frying pan over a high heat. Add the halloumi and apple slices to the pan and cook until they become golden, turning once halfway through. Sprinkle the apples with cinnamon. Serve the halloumi and apple slices onto plates and enjoy.

Quinoa & Berry Porridge

Ingredients

75g (3oz) quinoa, cooked
50g (2oz) raspberries
50g (2oz) blueberries
250mls (8fl oz) soya milk
2 tablespoons pumpkin seeds
Sprinkling of cinnamon

SERVES
1

351
calories
per
serving

Method

Place the quinoa and soya milk in a saucepan. Bring to the boil and cook for 5 minutes. Sprinkle in the cinnamon. Serve into a bowl, topped off with raspberries, blueberries and pumpkin seeds.

Tofu & Red Pepper Scramble

Ingredients

225g (8oz) tofu, diced
150g (5oz) kale leaves, finely chopped
1/2 red onion, finely sliced
1/2 red pepper (bell pepper), finely sliced
1/2 teaspoon ground cumin
1/2 teaspoon chilli powder
1/2 teaspoon turmeric
1/2 teaspoon sea salt
1/2 teaspoon garlic powder
2 tablespoon olive oil

SERVES 2

245 calories per serving

Method

Pat the tofu with a paper towel and let it drain for 10 minutes. Place the cumin, chilli, garlic, turmeric and salt in a bowl with a tablespoon of olive oil and mix it well. Heat a tablespoon of olive oil in a saucepan, add the kale, red pepper (bell pepper) and onion and cook the vegetables for 5 minutes. Stir in the tofu and pour over the spice mixture. Cook for 6-8 minutes until the tofu is golden. Serve and enjoy.

45

Apple Soufflé Omelette

Ingredients

2 eggs
1 apple, peeled, cored and chopped
½ tablespoon olive oil

SERVES
1

246
calories
per
serving

Method

Heat the apple with 2-3 tablespoons of water, until it becomes soft and pulpy and then set it aside. Separate the egg yolks from the whites and whisk the whites into soft peaks. Beat the yolks then fold them into the mixture.

Quick Blueberry Porridge

Ingredients

75g (3oz) porridge oats
75g (3oz) blueberries
200mls (7fl oz) unsweetened soya milk

SERVES
1

368
calories
per
serving

Method

Place the oats and soya milk into a saucepan and cook until the mixture thickens. Serve into a bowl and top it off with the berries. Enjoy.

LUNCH

Orange & Kale Salad

Ingredients

100g (3½ oz) kale, washed and finely chopped

1 orange, peeled, segmented and chopped

1 tablespoon roasted pistachio nuts

Juice of ½ lemon

1 tablespoon olive oil

SERVES 1

365 calories per serving

Method

Place the kale in a bowl and add in the lemon juice, olive oil and mix well then allow it to stand for 5 minutes. Add in the chopped orange and pistachio nuts and serve.

Mushroom & Red Wine Pâté

Ingredients

350g (12oz) mushrooms
2 onions, finely chopped
50g (2oz) fromage frais
1 clove garlic, chopped
1 teaspoon fresh parsley
150mls (5fl oz) red wine
1 tablespoon olive oil

SERVES 4

107 calories per serving

Method

Heat the oil in a saucepan, add the garlic and onion and cook for 5 minutes until softened. Stir in the mushrooms and cook for 4 minutes. Pour in the red wine and add the parsley. Bring to the boil, reduce the heat and simmer until the liquid has been absorbed. Remove from the heat and allow to cool. Once the mushroom mixture is completely cold, stir in the fromage frais. Transfer the pâté to a bowl and serve.

Carrot & Orange Soup

Ingredients

450g (1lb) carrots, chopped
3 tablespoons fresh parsley, plus extra
for garnish
2 onions, chopped
1 courgette (zucchini)
1 tablespoon olive oil
1200mls (2 pints) hot water
Grated zest and juice of 1 orange

SERVES 4

116 calories per serving

Method

Heat the oil in a saucepan, add the onion and cook for 5 minutes. Add in the carrots and courgette (zucchini) and cook for 5 minutes. Stir in the orange zest and hot water. Reduce the heat and simmer for 10 minutes. Stir in the parsley and orange juice. Using a hand blender or food processor blend the soup until smooth. Re-heat if necessary before serving. Serve with a sprinkling of parsley.

Miso Soup

Ingredients

225g (8oz) pak choi (bok choy), chopped
200g (7oz) tofu, cubed
10 spring onions (scallions), finely chopped
50g (2oz) red miso
1 tablespoon fresh coriander (cilantro), chopped
1 cm (½ inch) chunk of fresh ginger root, very finely chopped
1 small red chilli
2 tablespoons soy sauce (low sodium)
1200mls (2 pints) vegetable stock (broth)

SERVES 4

108 calories per serving

Method

Place the pak choi (bok choy), ginger, chilli and vegetable stock (broth) into a saucepan. Bring to the boil, reduce the heat and simmer for 10 minutes. Add the spring onions (scallions), tofu and soy sauce. Cook for 4 minutes. In a bowl, mix together the red miso with a few tablespoons of the soup then stir the miso into the soup. Stir in the coriander (cilantro) and serve.

Lemon & Rice Soup

Ingredients

100g (3½ oz) rice
3 courgettes (zucchinis), grated (shredded)
3 tablespoons fresh parsley, chopped
1 onion, chopped
1 clove garlic, chopped
900mls (1½ pints) vegetable stock (broth)
Zest and juice of 1 lemon
Sea salt
Freshly ground black pepper

SERVES 4

84 calories per serving

Method

Place the stock (broth) onion, rice, garlic and parsley into a pan and bring it to the boil. Reduce the heat and simmer for 35 minutes. Stir in the courgettes (zucchinis) and cook for 5 minutes. Add in the lemon zest and juice, salt and pepper. Serve and enjoy

Celeriac & Apple Soup

Ingredients

4 apples, peeled, cored and chopped
2 tablespoons fresh parsley, chopped
2½ cm (1 inch) chunk fresh root ginger
450g (1lb) celeriac, peeled and chopped
1 onion, chopped
600mls (1 pint) vegetable stock (broth)
1 tablespoon olive oil
Sea salt
Freshly ground black pepper

SERVES 4

151 calories per serving

Method

Heat the olive oil in a saucepan, add the onion and cook gently for 5 minutes. Add in the celeriac, apples, ginger and stock (broth). Bring to the boil, reduce the heat and cook for 20-25 minutes and the celeriac is tender. Use a hand blender or food processor and blitz until smooth. You can add hot water to make it thinner if you wish. Sprinkle in the parsley and season with salt and pepper.

Kale & Butterbean Soup

Ingredients

200g (7oz) kale
125g (4oz) butter beans
2 carrots, peeled and diced
1 stick celery
1 medium onion, peeled and chopped
1 clove of garlic, crushed
1 teaspoon olive oil
600mls (1 pint) vegetable stock (broth)
Sea salt
Freshly ground black pepper

SERVES 4

97 calories per serving

Method

Heat the olive oil in a large saucepan and add all of the vegetables apart from the kale and butterbeans. Stir for 2-3 minutes on a medium heat. Add the stock (broth) and bring to boil. Reduce and cook for 15 minutes. Blend half the butter beans and add to the soup. Add the kale, the remaining butter beans and cook for 10 minutes. This soup can be blended smooth or left chunky if you prefer. Season with salt and pepper then serve.

Quinoa & Parsley Cakes

Ingredients

100g (3½ oz) quinoa, cooked
50g (2oz) grated Cheddar cheese
25g (1oz) fresh whole-wheat breadcrumbs
2 eggs
1 small onion, finely chopped
4 tablespoons fresh parsley, chopped
1 tablespoon olive oil
Sea salt
Freshly ground black pepper

SERVES 2

324 calories per serving

Method

Place the eggs in a large bowl and whisk. Add the onion, parsley, cheese, breadcrumbs and season with salt and pepper. Mix well. Add the cooked quinoa and combine with the other ingredients. Heat the olive oil in a large frying pan. With clean hands, form 8 small patties. Place them in the frying pan and cook for about 3 minutes on each side or until golden brown.

Roast Courgettes (Zucchinis) & Olives

Ingredients

12 olives
4 medium courgettes (zucchinis), thickly sliced lengthways
2 tablespoons olive oil
Sea salt
Freshly ground black pepper

SERVES 4

100 calories per serving

Method

Place the courgette (zucchini) slices in an ovenproof dish and scatter over the olives. Drizzle them with olive oil and season with salt and pepper. Transfer them to the oven and bake at 200C/400F for 15 minutes, turning halfway through.

Avocado & Orange Salad

Ingredients

2 large avocados, de-stoned and peeled
3 oranges
12g (½ oz) cardamom pods
200g (7oz) fresh watercress
1 tablespoon olive oil
½ teaspoon ground allspice
Juice of ½ lime

SERVES 4

236 calories per serving

Method

Cut the orange flesh from the outer skin to remove the individual segments and place them in a bowl. Slice the avocados and add them to the orange segments. Using the back of a spoon or a mortar and pestle, break the cardamom pods open and remove the tiny seeds. In a bowl, mix together the cardamom seeds with the lime juice, olive oil and allspice. Toss the oranges, avocados and watercress in the dressing then serve.

Kale & Bacon

Ingredients

250g (9oz) fresh kale, finely chopped
8 rashers of back bacon
2 cloves of garlic, crushed
1 tablespoon olive oil
Sea salt
Freshly ground black pepper

SERVES 4

197 calories per serving

Method

Heat the olive oil in a saucepan, add the bacon and cook until brown. Add in the garlic and kale and cook for 5-6 minutes or until the kale has wilted. Season with salt and pepper. Serve.

Garlic & Herb King Prawns

SERVES 4

157 calories per serving

Ingredients

450g (1lb) king prawns
4 tablespoons fresh parsley, chopped
3 cloves of garlic, crushed
2 tablespoons olive oil
Juice of 1 lemon

Method

In a bowl, place a tablespoon of olive oil, parsley, lemon juice and garlic. Add the prawns and coat them with the mixture. Place in the fridge and marinate for 30 minutes, or longer if possible. When you're ready to cook the prawns, heat a tablespoon of olive oil in a pan. Add the prawns and cook them until for around 3-4 minutes until they are cooked through and completely pink. Serve and enjoy.

Pork & Apple Burgers

Ingredients

450g (1lb) pork mince (ground pork)
25g (1oz) Cheddar cheese, grated (shredded)
4 iceberg lettuce leaves
1 large apple, peeled, cored and finely chopped
1 egg, beaten
1 tablespoon fresh parsley, chopped
1 small onion, finely chopped
Freshly ground black pepper

SERVES 4

248 calories per serving

Method

In a bowl combine the pork, onion, apple, cheese, egg and parsley. Season with pepper. Shape the burger mixture into patties. Place them under a hot grill (broiler) for around 6 minutes on each side until completely cooked through. Instead of a bread bun wrap each burger in a lettuce leave and serve.

60

Chilli & Lime Mackerel

Ingredients

2 mackerel fillets
1 tablespoon fresh coriander (cilantro), chopped
1 red chilli, de-seeded and chopped
1/2 teaspoon ground coriander (cilantro)
1/2 teaspoon ground cumin
Zest and juice of 1 lime
1 tablespoon olive oil

SERVES 2

310 calories per serving

Method

Place the cumin, fresh and ground coriander (cilantro), chilli, zest and juice of the lime and olive oil in a bowl and mix well. Thickly coat the mackerel with the mixture. Transfer the fish to a hot grill (broiler) and cook for around 4 minutes on each side until cooked through.

Prawns & Lemon Quinoa

Ingredients

- 200g (7oz) quinoa, cooked
- 450g (1lb) raw prawns, shelled
- 400g (14oz) butter beans, rinsed and drained
- 2 tablespoons capers
- 2 tablespoons fresh parsley, chopped
- 25g (1oz) butter
- ½ teaspoon paprika
- Juice of 1 lemon
- 3 tablespoons olive oil

SERVES 4

373 calories per serving

Method

In a hot pan, heat 2 tablespoons of the oil. Add the prawns and paprika and fry for 3-4 minutes until cooked through. Transfer to a plate and set aside. Put the beans, capers, butter and lemon juice in the pan and cook for 2 minutes. Add the parsley and the remaining olive oil to the pan and stir. Finally, add the quinoa and combine. Season and serve the quinoa topped with the paprika prawns.

Spicy Edamame (Soy Beans)

Ingredients

- 400g (14oz) edamame (soy beans), frozen or fresh
- 400g (14oz) tinned chopped tomatoes
- 4 shallots, chopped
- 2cm (1inch) chunk fresh root ginger
- 2 teaspoons garam masala
- 1 tablespoon olive oil

SERVES
4

259
calories
per
serving

Method

Heat the olive oil in a frying pan, add the shallots and cook for 3 minutes. Stir in the ginger and garam masala then add the chopped tomatoes. Cook for 4 minutes. Add the edamame and heat them thoroughly. Serve and enjoy.

Kale Chips

Ingredients

- 200g (7oz) fresh kale
- 2 tablespoons olive oil
- Sea salt
- Freshly ground black pepper

SERVES
4

78
calories
per
serving

Method

Remove the stalks from the kale and cut the leaves into bite-size squares, of around 4cms (2 inches). Put the oil, pepper and salt into a bowl and coat the kale leaves. Scatter them on to a baking sheet, transfer them to the oven and bake at 170C/325F for around 10 minutes or until crispy.

SuperFood Green Salad

Ingredients

2 avocados, de-stoned, peeled and chopped
150g (5oz) broccoli, broken into florets
75g (3oz) spinach leaves
75g (3oz) kale, finely chopped
25g (1oz) pumpkin seeds
25g (1oz) sesame seeds
25g (1oz) sunflower seeds
2 tablespoons soy sauce
2 tablespoons fresh coriander (cilantro) chopped

FOR THE DRESSING:
3 tablespoons olive oil
1 teaspoon honey
Juice of 1 lemon
Sea salt
Freshly ground black pepper

SERVES 4

382 calories per serving

Method

Place the pumpkin, sesame and sunflower seeds in a frying pan and dry fry for 2-3 minutes until slightly toasted. Transfer them to a bowl and add in the soy sauce then set aside. Steam the broccoli for 5 minutes or until tender. Transfer the broccoli to a serving bowl and allow it to cool. Add in the kale, spinach, avocado and coriander (cilantro) and stir. Pour in the dressing and mix well. Sprinkle the seeds into the salad. Serve and eat immediately.

Feta Cheese & Orange Salad

Ingredients

4 tomatoes, quartered
4 spring onions (scallions), chopped
2 oranges, peeled and segmented
75g (3oz) black olives
125g (4oz) feta cheese, crumbled
2 tablespoons fresh coriander (cilantro)
2 tablespoons olive oil
Juice of 1 lime
Sea salt
Freshly ground black pepper

SERVES 4

197 calories per serving

Method

Place the tomatoes, spring onions (scallions), olives, feta, coriander (cilantro). Stir in the lime juice and olive oil. Season with salt and pepper. Add in the oranges and serve.

Lime Tofu & Rice Noodle Salad

Ingredients

300g (11oz) tofu, diced

200g (7oz) rice noodles

100g (3½ oz) mange tout (snow peas), chopped

8 radishes, chopped

3 tablespoon soy sauce

2 tablespoon sesame seeds

2 tablespoons fresh coriander (cilantro) chopped

1 red onion, finely chopped

1 red chilli, deseeded and finely chopped

Juice of 1 lime

SERVES 4

225 calories per serving

Method

Place the tofu in a bowl and add in the soy sauce, lime juice, chilli and allow it to marinate for an hour. Cook the rice noodles according to the manufacturer's instructions. Place the noodles, radishes, mange tout, onion and sesame seeds in a bowl then add in the marinated tofu and fresh coriander (cilantro) leaves. Serve and enjoy.

Fennel & Grapefruit Quinoa Salad

Ingredients

- 225g (8oz) quinoa
- 225g (8oz) fennel, finely chopped
- 2 spring onions (scallions), chopped
- 2 tablespoons fresh parsley, chopped
- 2 grapefruits, peeled and segmented
- 900mls (1½ pints) vegetable stock (broth)
- 3 tablespoons olive oil
- Juice of ½ lemon

SERVES 4

204 calories per serving

Method

Pour the stock (broth) into a saucepan, bring it to the boil and add the quinoa. Cook for around 10 minutes until the grains have opened up. Drain and set aside to cool down. Place the grapefruit, fennel, spring onions (scallions) and parsley into a bowl and stir in the quinoa. Add in the lemon juice, olive oil and mix thoroughly. Serve chilled.

Kale, Blue Cheese & Walnut Salad

Ingredients

200g (7oz) kale leaves, finely chopped and thick stalks removed
100g (3½ oz) blue cheese, crumbled
12 walnut halves
2 tablespoons fresh parsley, chopped
2 tablespoons olive oil
2 tablespoons apple cider vinegar

SERVES 4

277 calories per serving

Method

Mix the vinegar, olive oil, kale and parsley in a bowl and coat the leaves well. Add the walnuts and blue cheese to the salad and serve.

Lemon Baked Asparagus

Ingredients

225g (8oz) asparagus spears, trimmed
2 tablespoons olive oil
Juice of 1 lemon

SERVES 2

164 calories per serving

Method

Lay out the asparagus spears on a baking tray. Mix together the olive oil and lemon juice then pour it over the asparagus. Place it in the oven at 200C/400F for 12 minutes, turning the asparagus over half way through cooking. Serve and eat.

Chorizo, Kale & Spinach Salad

Ingredients

- 100g (3½ oz) spinach
- 100g (3½ oz) kale leaves, chopped
- 75g (3oz) chorizo sausage, thinly sliced
- 2 tablespoons olive oil
- 2 tablespoons white wine vinegar
- Sea salt
- Freshly ground black pepper

SERVES 2

300 calories per serving

Method

Remove any thick stalks from the spinach. Pour the olive oil into a frying pan and add the sliced chorizo. Cook for around 3 minutes. Add the spinach, kale and white wine vinegar. Cook until the vegetables have wilted. Season with salt and pepper. Serve immediately.

69

Zesty Quinoa Salad

Ingredients

225g (8oz) quinoa, cooked
1 small red onion, finely chopped
6 cherry tomatoes, quartered
1 apple, peeled, cored and chopped
½ cucumber, diced
2 tablespoons fresh parsley, finely chopped
6 pitted olives, finely chopped
2 cloves garlic, crushed
2 tablespoons olive oil
Juice of 1 lemon
¼ teaspoon sea salt
¼ teaspoon freshly ground black pepper

SERVES 2

332 calories per serving

Method

In a large bowl, mix together the garlic, olive oil, lemon juice, salt, and pepper. Add the quinoa, red onion, apple, tomatoes, cucumber, olives, and parsley. Toss all the ingredients in the dressing until it's thoroughly coated. Cover and chill in the fridge before serving.

DINNER

Pesto Salmon & Courgette 'Spaghetti'

Ingredients

1 tablespoon pesto sauce
2 medium salmon fillets
2 medium courgettes (zucchinis)
1 tablespoon olive oil
Juice of 1 lemon

SERVES 2

397 calories per serving

Method

Evenly coat the salmon fillets in the pesto sauce. Heat the olive oil in a frying pan. Cook the salmon for 4-5 minutes on each side until the fish changes colour. In the meantime, use a vegetable peeler and peel thin strips off the courgette (zucchini). Remove the salmon from the pan and keep warm. If necessary, add a little extra oil to the frying pan. Place the courgette strips into the pan and cook for 2-3 minutes until soft. Serve the courgette spaghetti onto plates and place the salmon on top with a squeeze of lemon juice on each.

Slow-Cooked Chicken & Butternut Squash

Ingredients

150g (5oz) butternut squash, chopped
4 medium chicken breasts
3 garlic cloves, crushed
6cm (3 inch) chunk of root ginger, peeled and sliced
2 x 400g (2 x 14oz) tins chopped tomatoes
2 teaspoons ground cumin
2 teaspoons ground cinnamon
1 teaspoon turmeric
1 onion, chopped
1 tablespoon olive oil

SERVES 4

290 calories per serving

Method

In a large bowl combine the cumin, turmeric and cinnamon, add the chicken and coat it thoroughly. Heat the oil in a saucepan and add the chicken and cook for 5 minutes until slightly golden. In a slow cooker, place the onion, garlic and ginger. Add chicken then top it off with tomatoes and squash. Cover and slow cook on high until the chicken is cooked through and tender.

73

Swordfish With Lemon & Parsley

SERVES 2

314 calories per serving

Ingredients

2 x 150g (2 x 5oz) swordfish steaks
50g (2oz) spinach leaves
2 tablespoons fresh parsley, chopped
2 tablespoons olive oil
1 clove of garlic
Juice of 1 lemon
Freshly ground black pepper

Method

Mix together the lemon juice, 2 tablespoons olive oil, garlic and parsley and season with pepper. Place the fish on a plate and lightly coat it with a tablespoon of the lemon & parsley mixture. Heat a frying pan and add the swordfish steaks. Cook for 3-4 minutes on each side and check that it's completely cooked. Scatter the spinach leaves onto plates. Serve the fish on top and spoon over the remaining lemon and parsley dressing. Enjoy.

Chicken & Red Wine Casserole

Ingredients

400g (14oz) small new potatoes
400g (14oz) tinned chopped tomatoes
12 black olives
4 chicken breasts, roughly chopped
4 stalks rosemary
300mls (1/2 pint) red wine
600mls (1 pint) chicken stock (broth)
1oz (25g) capers
2 teaspoons fresh parsley, chopped
1 teaspoon honey
1 tablespoon olive oil
Zest and juice of 1 orange
Sea salt, freshly ground black pepper

SERVES 4

390 calories per serving

Method

Heat the olive oil in a frying pan add the chicken and brown it for a few minutes. Add in the potatoes, red wine, chicken stock (broth) tomatoes, garlic, rosemary and honey and bring it to the boil. Reduce the heat and simmer for 1 hour or alternatively transfer it to a slow cooker and cook until tender. At the end of cooking stir in the orange zest, juice, capers, parsley and olives and season with salt and pepper. Remove the rosemary stalks and serve.

Bean & Vegetable Tagine

Ingredients

- 400g (14oz) brown rice
- 400g (14oz) cannellini beans
- 150g (5oz) mushrooms, chopped
- 50g (2oz) dried apricots, chopped
- 3 carrots, chopped
- 3 tomatoes, chopped
- 3 cloves of garlic, crushed
- 3 tablespoons coriander (cilantro), chopped
- 2 teaspoons ground cumin
- 2 teaspoons ground coriander (cilantro)
- 1 medium aubergine (eggplant), chopped
- 1 large onion, chopped
- 1 teaspoon turmeric
- 600mls (1 pint) vegetable stock (broth)
- 1 tablespoon olive oil

SERVES 4

349 calories per serving

Method

Heat the olive oil in a large saucepan. Add the onion and garlic and cook for 4 minutes. Sprinkle in the spices and stir. Add the aubergine (eggplant), cannellini beans, tomatoes, carrots and mushrooms and cook for 5 minutes. Add the apricots. Pour in the vegetable stock (broth), bring to the boil then reduce the heat and simmer for 20 minutes until the vegetables have softened. In the meantime cook the brown rice according to the manufacturers instructions. When the tagine has cooked, stir in the coriander (cilantro). Drain the rice and serve it with the tagine.

Creole Chicken

Ingredients

- 400g (14oz) brown rice
- 4 chicken breasts
- 250g (9 oz) mange tout (snow peas)
- 2 x 400g (2 x 14oz) tinned chopped tomatoes
- 4 cloves garlic, chopped
- 1 onion, chopped
- 3 teaspoons curry powder
- 1 teaspoon ground cumin
- 1/2 teaspoon paprika
- 200mls (7fl oz) chicken stock (broth)
- 1 tablespoon olive oil

SERVES 4

416 calories per serving

Method

Heat the oil in a frying pan, add the chicken, cumin, paprika and curry powder and cook until the chicken is browned. Add the onion, garlic, tomatoes and cook for 4 minutes. Pour in the stock (broth), bring it the boil then reduce the heat and simmer for 25 minutes. In the meantime cook the brown rice according to the instructions. Stir the mange tout (snow peas) into the creole chicken and cook for 5 minutes. Serve the chicken alongside the rice.

Scallops With Garlic & Herb Butter

Ingredients

50g (2oz) butter
400g (4oz) large scallops, shelled
2 tablespoons fresh parsley, finely chopped
2 cloves of garlic, crushed
1 lemon, quartered
1 tablespoon olive oil
Sea salt
Freshly ground black pepper

SERVES 4

206 calories per serving

Method

Place the olive oil in a frying pan over a high heat. Add the scallops and cook for around 1 minute on either side until they are slightly golden. Transfer to a dish and keep warm. Drain off any excess liquid from the pan. Gently warm the butter and the garlic for around 1 minute until the butter has melted, add the lemon juice then sprinkle in the fresh parsley. Serve the scallops and pour over the parsley butter. It's simple and delicious.

Pork with Kale & Pomegranate

Ingredients

450g (1lb) pork steaks, cut into strips
75g (3oz) kale, finely chopped
2 tablespoons fresh parsley, finely chopped
1 tablespoon olive oil
2 cloves of garlic
Seeds of 1 pomegranate
Sea salt
Freshly ground black pepper
FOR THE DRESSING:
2 tablespoons walnuts, chopped
3 tablespoons olive oil
Juice of 1 lemon

SERVES 4

454 calories per serving

Method

Place the ingredients for the dressing into a bowl and mix them together. Place the kale, parsley and pomegranate seeds in a bowl and mix together with the dressing then set aside. Heat the olive oil in a frying pan, add the pork strips and cook for 8-10 minutes, stirring occasionally until thoroughly cooked. Scatter the kale and pomegranate mixture onto a serving plate and add the cooked pork strips on top. Season with salt and pepper then serve.

Roast Chicken & Chorizo

Ingredients

400g (14oz) chicken thighs
400g (14oz) chopped tomatoes
150g (5oz) chorizo sausage, chopped
100g (3 ½ oz) kale, chopped
2 cloves of garlic, crushed
1 onion, sliced
1 tablespoon parsley
25g (1oz) capers
200mls (7fl oz) chicken stock (broth)
1 tablespoon olive oil
Sea salt
Freshly ground black pepper

SERVES 4

455 calories per serving

Method

Heat a tablespoon of olive oil in a large saucepan, add the chicken and brown it until the skin is crispy. Transfer the chicken to a casserole dish. Add the chorizo, onion, garlic, tomatoes and kale. Pour in a tablespoon of olive oil and coat the ingredients well. Season with salt and pepper. Cover the casserole dish with foil. Bake it in the oven for 30 minutes then remove the foil, add the capers and cook for another 5 minutes. Sprinkle with parsley and serve.

Mild Vegetable Curry

Ingredients

400g (14oz) brown rice
250g (9 oz) mushrooms, chopped
250g (9 oz) tofu, cubed
125g (4oz) green beans
2 teaspoons mild curry powder
1 tablespoon fresh coriander (cilantro)
1 teaspoon cumin
1 teaspoon turmeric
400mls (14fl oz) coconut milk

SERVES 4

377 calories per serving

Method

Warm the coconut milk in a saucepan then add in the curry powder, cumin and turmeric and mix it well. Add the green beans, mushrooms, tofu and stir. Bring it to the boil, reduce the heat and simmer for 6-7 minutes until the vegetables are soft. In the meantime cook the rice according to the instructions. Serve the vegetable curry on a bed of rice and sprinkle with coriander (cilantro) before serving.

Vegetarian Hot Pot

Ingredients

400g (14oz) haricot beans
400g (14oz) black-eyed beans
400g (14oz) tinned chopped tomatoes
225g (8oz) mushrooms, sliced
2 onions, finely chopped
2 cloves of garlic, chopped
1 tablespoon paprika
4 tablespoons fresh parsley
250mls (8fl oz) vegetable stock (broth)
1 tablespoon olive oil
1 tablespoon soy sauce
Sea salt
Freshly ground black pepper

SERVES 4

251 calories per serving

Method

Heat the oil in a saucepan, add the garlic and onions and cook for 4 minutes. Add in the mushrooms, haricot beans, black-eyed peas, tomatoes, paprika and soy sauce. Stir and cook for 5 minutes. Add in the stock (broth) and simmer for 15 minutes. Stir in the parsley, season with salt and pepper then serve and enjoy.

Rosemary & Lemon Lamb

Ingredients

225g (8oz) green beans
225g (8oz) asparagus
4 medium sized lamb chump chops
4 sprigs of rosemary, stalk removed and leaves finely chopped
4 cloves of garlic, crushed
4 tablespoons fresh parsley, finely chopped
Grated zest of 2 lemons
3 tablespoons olive oil

SERVES 4

336 calories per serving

Method

Place the lemon zest, parsley, rosemary, garlic and 2 tablespoons of olive oil in a bowl and mix well. Pour half of the marinade over the lamb and allow it to marinate for at least an hour, or overnight if you can. Heat a tablespoon of oil in a frying pan; add the lamb and cook for around 5 minutes on each side, or until it's cooked to your liking. In the meantime, steam the asparagus and green beans for 5-6 minutes. Serve the vegetables onto plates, place the lamb chops on top and drizzle over the oily marinade.

Lemon & Lime Lentil Salad

Ingredients

- 200g (7oz) Puy lentils
- 4 eggs
- 4 large tomatoes, deseeded and chopped
- 4 spring onions (scallions), finely chopped
- 2 tablespoons olive oil
- 2 tablespoons parsley
- 50g (2oz) spinach leaves
- 1 clove of garlic
- Juice and rind of 1 lemon
- Sea salt
- Freshly ground black pepper

SERVES 4

228 calories per serving

Method

Place the lentils in a saucepan, cover them with water and bring them to the boil. Reduce the heat and cook for 20-25 minutes. Drain them once they are soft. Heat the olive oil in a saucepan, add the garlic and spring onions (scallions) and cook for 2 minutes. Stir in the tomatoes, lemon juice and rind. Cook for 2 minutes. Stir in the lentils and keep warm. In a pan of gently simmering water, poach the eggs until they are set but soft in the middle which should be 3-4 minutes. Scatter the spinach leaves onto plates, serve the lentils and top off with a poached egg. Season with salt and pepper.

Ginger & Orange Salmon Stir-Fry

Ingredients

- 200g (7oz) kale, finely chopped
- 4 salmon steaks, skin removed
- 5cm (2 inch) fresh root ginger, finely chopped
- 3 cloves of garlic, crushed
- 1 red chilli, de-seeded and chopped
- 1 red onion, finely chopped
- 5 tablespoons hot water
- 3 tablespoons soy sauce
- 1 tablespoon olive oil
- Freshly squeezed juice of 1 orange

SERVES 4

353 calories per serving

Method

Place the half of the ginger, garlic and chilli into a bowl with a tablespoon of soy sauce and mix well. Coat the salmon in the mixture. Transfer it to a hot grill (broiler) and cook for 10 minutes, turning once half way through. Heat the oil in a hot wok or frying pan, add the chopped onion and cook for 4-5 minutes or until tender. Add in the hot water, kale and the remaining ginger, garlic and chilli. Cook for 4-5 minutes or until the kale has wilted. Stir in the orange juice and 2 tablespoons soy sauce. Serve and enjoy.

Creamy Chicken Curry

Ingredients

650g (1 ½lb) chicken breasts, chopped
5 cloves garlic, chopped
2 teaspoons turmeric
3 teaspoons medium curry powder
1 teaspoon ground cumin
1 onion, chopped
1 red pepper (bell pepper), chopped
1 handful of coriander (cilantro) chopped
400mls (14fl oz) coconut milk
1 tablespoon olive oil

SERVES 4-6

389 calories per serving

Method

Heat the olive oil in a saucepan, add the onion and cook it for 5 minutes. Stir in the garlic and the chicken and cook it for 7-8 minutes. Add the turmeric, curry powder and cumin and mix well. Pour in the coconut milk and add in the red pepper (bell pepper) and coriander (cilantro). Bring it to the boil, reduce the heat and simmer for around 10 minutes. Serve with cauliflower rice, which is a great low calorie, low carb alternative to ordinary rice. See recipe on page 87.

Curried Cauliflower Rice

Ingredients

- 1 medium cauliflower, approx 900g (2lb)
- 1 tablespoon olive oil
- ½ teaspoon ground cumin
- ½ teaspoon curry powder
- Sea salt
- Freshly ground black pepper

SERVES 6

66 calories per serving

Method

Place the cauliflower into a food processor and chop until fine, similar to rice. Heat the olive oil in a frying pan. Stir in the cumin, curry powder and the cauliflower. Cook for 6-7 minutes or until softened. Season with salt and pepper. Serve as an alternative to rice.

Cheese Stuffed Meatballs

Ingredients

250g (9oz) lean minced steak (ground beef)
50g (2oz) mozzarella, cut into chunks
1 tablespoon fresh basil, finely chopped
1 tablespoon fresh parsley, finely chopped
2 cloves garlic, crushed
1 tablespoon olive oil
Freshly ground black pepper

SERVES 2

386 calories per serving

Method

In a bowl, combine the minced steak (ground beef), garlic, basil, parsley and black pepper then divide the mixture into 4 and shape it into round balls. With your finger make a hold in the middle of each ball and press a chunk of mozzarella into the meatball then cover and seal it over with the meat. Heat the olive oil in a frying pan, add the burgers and quickly brown them for about 1 minute on each side. Reduce the heat and cook for around 3 minutes turning to ensure they are thoroughly cooked.

Roast Courgettes (Zucchinis) & Olives

Ingredients

6 olives
2 courgettes (zucchinis), thickly sliced lengthways
1 tablespoon olive oil
Sea salt
Freshly ground black pepper

SERVES 2

99 calories per serving

Method

Place the courgette (zucchini) slices in an ovenproof dish and scatter over the olives. Drizzle with olive oil and season with salt and pepper. Transfer them to the oven and bake at 200C/400F for 15 minutes, turning halfway through.

Feta, Almond & Quinoa Salad

Ingredients

300g (11oz) quinoa
125g (4oz) feta cheese
50g (2oz) flaked almonds
1 teaspoon ground coriander (cilantro)
1 teaspoon turmeric
2 tablespoons coriander (cilantro) leaves, chopped
2 tablespoons fresh parsley, chopped
600mls (1 pint) hot water
1 tablespoon olive oil
Juice of 1 lime
Sea salt
Freshly ground black pepper

SERVES 4

442 calories per serving

Method

Heat the olive oil in a large frying pan, add the ground coriander (cilantro) and turmeric and stir. Add in the quinoa and mix it with the spices. Pour in the hot water, stir and simmer for around 12 minutes or until the quinoa grains have opened out. Remove it from the heat. Stir in the feta cheese, almond flakes, parsley, coriander (cilantro) leaves and the lime juice. Season with salt and pepper. Serve and enjoy.

Spiced Turkey Burgers

Ingredients

450g (1lb) minced (ground) turkey
75g (3oz) fresh coriander (cilantro), finely chopped
2 teaspoons curry powder
2 garlic cloves, crushed
1 onion, finely chopped
½ teaspoon chilli flakes
1 tablespoon olive oil
Sea salt
Freshly ground black pepper

SERVES 4

182 calories per serving

Method

Place the turkey in a large bowl, add the coriander (cilantro), curry powder, garlic, onion and chilli flakes and combine the ingredients well. Season with salt and pepper. Divide the mixture into 4 and form into burger shapes. Heat the olive oil in a frying pan. Place the burgers in the pan and cook for around 7- 8 minutes on either side until the burgers are cooked thoroughly.

Balsamic Roast Vegetables

Ingredients

- 4 cloves garlic, chopped
- 2 medium aubergines (eggplants), sliced
- 450g (1lb) butternut squash, peeled de-seeded and chopped
- 1 red pepper (bell pepper), sliced
- 1 green pepper (bell pepper), sliced
- 1 yellow pepper (bell pepper) sliced
- 1 onion, chopped
- 1 teaspoon ground coriander (cilantro)
- 1 teaspoon ground cumin
- 1 handful of fresh basil, chopped
- 1 handful of fresh parsley, chopped
- 2 tablespoons balsamic vinegar
- 2 tablespoons olive oil

SERVES 4

175 calories per serving

Method

Place all of the vegetables into a roasting tin and sprinkle in the cumin, coriander (cilantro), olive oil, garlic and balsamic vinegar. Apart from the fresh herbs, toss everything together and make sure it's well coated. Roast in the oven at 220C/425F for 25-30 minutes or until the vegetables have softened and are caramelised. Stir in the fresh herbs. Delicious with a green leafy salad.

Chicken, Kale & Sweet Potato Pie

Ingredients

450g (1lb) sweet potatoes, peeled and sliced
450g (1lb) minced (ground) chicken
1 tablespoon olive oil
1 onion, chopped finely
2 carrots, chopped
1 tablespoon fresh parsley
600mls (1 pint) chicken stock (broth)
150g (5oz) kale
1 garlic clove, crushed
1 teaspoon plain flour (all-purpose flour)
25g (1oz) butter
Sea salt and pepper

SERVES 4

447 calories per serving

Method

Heat the olive oil in a pan and fry the chicken mince for 7 minutes. Transfer it to a bowl. Add the kale, onion and carrots to the pan and fry until they soften. Add the parsley and garlic. Cook for 1 minute. Sprinkle in the flour and stir well then add the chicken stock (broth). Add the chicken to the pan, reduce the heat and simmer for 10 minutes. Transfer the ingredients to an ovenproof casserole dish. Boil the sweet potatoes for 10-15 minutes, drain and mash them with the butter. Season with salt and pepper. Spoon the sweet potatoes over the chicken mixture. Bake in the oven at 200C/400F for 35-40 minutes until hot.

Orange Pork & Leeks

Ingredients

- 450g (1lb) pork chops
- 2 medium leeks, thinly sliced
- 1 red pepper (bell pepper) sliced
- 150mls (5fl oz) chicken stock (broth)
- 3 garlic cloves, crushed
- 1 tablespoon mustard
- 1/2 teaspoon paprika
- 1/4 teaspoon salt
- 1/4 teaspoon freshly ground black pepper
- 1 tablespoon olive oil
- Juice of 1 orange

SERVES 4

375 calories per serving

Method

Sprinkle the pork chops with salt, and black pepper. Heat the oil in a frying pan. Add the pork chops and fry for 3 minutes on each side or until cooked through. Remove the pork chops and keep them warm. Add to the pan the leeks, pepper (bell pepper), and garlic. Fry for 3 minutes until the leek has softened. Add in the stock (broth) orange juice, mustard, and paprika. Stir and cook for 2-3 minutes or until the liquid thickens slightly. Return the pork chops to the pan and coat them in the juices. Serve and enjoy.

Lamb Skewers & Onion Raita

Ingredients

450g (1lb) boneless lamb steaks
150g (5oz) plain (unflavoured) yogurt
2 teaspoons ground cumin
1 teaspoon turmeric
1 teaspoon ground coriander (cilantro)
Juice of 1 lemon
ONION RAITA
250g (9 oz) natural yogurt (unflavoured)
1 fresh mint, chopped
1 red onion, finely sliced
1/4 teaspoon cumin

SERVES 4

376 calories per serving

Method

Chop the lamb into bite-size chunks. In a bowl, combine the 150g (5oz) yogurt, cumin, turmeric, coriander (cilantro) and lemon juice. Add the lamb to the marinade, cover it and place it in the fridge for one hour. In the meantime, to make the raita, combine the 250g (9oz) yogurt, chopped onion, mint and cumin. Chill it in the fridge. Once the lamb is marinated, thread the lamb chunks onto skewers. Place under a hot grill (broiler) for 5 minutes on either side. Serve with the raita.

Kale & Coconut Dahl

Ingredients

125g (4oz) kale
450g (1lb) brown lentils
400ml (14fl oz) coconut milk
3 garlic cloves, chopped
2cm (1in) chunk of fresh ginger, peeled and finely chopped
2 teaspoons ground cumin
2 teaspoon ground coriander (cilantro)
2 tablespoons fresh coriander (cilantro), chopped
1 tomato, chopped
1 teaspoon chilli powder
1 onion, chopped
½ teaspoon turmeric
1 tablespoon olive oil

SERVES 4

300 calories per serving

Method

Heat the olive oil in a large saucepan. Add the onion, tomato, cumin, ginger, ground coriander (cilantro), chilli, turmeric, garlic and cook for about 10 minutes or until the onion is soft. Add the coconut milk and lentils. Cook for 20 minutes. Add the kale and stir. Cook for another 5 minutes. Just before serving, add the fresh coriander and stir. Serve with a salad or cauliflower rice.

Lemon Chicken Skewers

Ingredients

450g (1lb) chicken breast fillets, diced
2 garlic cloves, crushed
1 teaspoon ground cumin
1 tablespoon fresh coriander (cilantro), chopped
250g (9oz) plain (unflavoured) yogurt
Zest and juice of 1 lemon

SERVES 4

183 calories per serving

Method

Place the yogurt into a bowl and stir in the garlic, lemon zest and juice, cumin and coriander (cilantro). Add in the chopped chicken and mix well. Allow the chicken to marinate for at least 1 hour. Thread the chicken onto skewers. Place the skewers under a hot grill (broiler) or onto a barbecue and cook for around 4 minutes on each side until the chicken is thoroughly cooked.

Parma Chicken & Capers

Ingredients

- 4 chicken breasts
- 4 slices Parma ham
- 25g (1oz) capers, chopped
- 2 tablespoons fresh parsley, chopped
- 50g (2oz) butter
- 1 lemon, cut into slices

SERVES 4

314 calories per serving

Method

Cover the chicken breasts with cling film (plastic wrap). Using a rolling pin beat the chicken breasts until each one is flattened. Place the chicken breasts in an ovenproof dish and lay a slice of ham on top. In a bowl, combine the butter, capers and parsley. Place a scoop of the butter mixture on top of the Parma ham and add a slice of lemon. Transfer them to the oven and bake at 200C/400F for 25 minutes or until the chicken is cooked through.

DESSERTS, TREATS & SNACKS

Chocolate Mousse

Ingredients

75mls (3fl oz) double cream (heavy cream)
50g (2oz) cream cheese
25g (1oz) unsalted butter
1 tablespoon 100% cocoa powder
1 teaspoon stevia (or to taste)

SERVES 2

400 calories per serving

Method

Place the butter and stevia into a bowl and mix until smooth. Stir in the cream cheese and cocoa powder and mix thoroughly. Whip the cream until thick and fold it into the mixture. Spoon the mousse into long stemmed glasses or serving bowls. Chill before serving.

Chocolate & Hazelnut Clusters

Ingredients

125g (4oz) dark chocolate (min 70% cocoa)
125g (4oz) dates, chopped
50g (2oz) hazelnuts, chopped

Makes 24

58 calories per serving

Method

Place the chocolate into a bowl and place the bowl over a saucepan of simmering water. Once the chocolate has melted, remove it from the heat. Stir in the hazelnuts and dates. Spoon the mixture into small paper cases and allow it to set. Serve and enjoy.

Green Tea Tropical Fruit Salad

Ingredients

1 green tea teabag
225mls (8fl oz) hot water
225g (8oz) blueberries
1 cantaloupe melon, deseeded and chopped
1 papaya, deseeded and chopped
1 mango, stone removed and chopped
2 apples, peeled, cored and chopped
2 kiwi fruit, peeled and chopped
Seeds of 1 pomegranate

SERVES 4

205 calories per serving

Method

Pour the hot water into a cup, add the teabag and allow it to sit for 5 minutes. Set aside and allow it to cool. Place all of the fruit into a large bowl and combine it. Once the tea has cooled pour it onto the fruit salad and stir. Chill before serving.

Apple & Walnut Creams

Ingredients

100g (3 1/2 oz) cream cheese
50g (2oz) walnuts, roughly chopped
4 apples
3 tablespoons lemon juice

SERVES 4

221 calories per serving

Method

Peel and core the apples then slice them evenly width ways to create a circular shape. Lightly coat the apple slices in lemon juice and place them on a serving plate. Mix together the cream cheese and walnuts then spoon a little of the mixture onto each apple ring. Eat immediately.

Blueberry Mousse

Ingredients

200g (7oz) blueberries
125g (4oz) silken tofu

SERVES 2

78 calories per serving

Method

Place the blueberries in a small pan and simmer for 10-15 minutes or until they are completely soft. Set them aside to cool. Place the blueberries and tofu into a blender and process until smooth. Spoon it into glasses or bowls and chill before serving.

Fruit & Nut Bars

Ingredients

75g (3oz) blueberries
75g (3oz) almonds, roughly chopped
350g (12oz) dark chocolate, minimum 70% cocoa

Makes 16

156 calories per serving

Method

Line a shallow baking tin with greaseproof paper. Place the chocolate in a bowl and place it over a saucepan of gently simmering water. Stir gently while the chocolate melts. Scatter the blueberries and almonds over the baking sheet then pour on the melted chocolate. Cover and chill in the fridge for around an hour. Cut into 16 pieces and serve.

Banana & Blueberry Rice Pudding

Ingredients

150g (5oz) risotto rice
50g (2oz) dried bananas
100g (3½ oz) fresh blueberries
1 vanilla pod, split open
1 litre (1½ pints) unsweetened soya milk

SERVES 4

302 calories per serving

Method

Place the milk into saucepan and add the rice, bananas and vanilla pod. Bring it to the boil, reduce the heat and simmer for 15 minutes until the rice is soft. Remove the vanilla pod and stir in the blueberries. Serve the pudding immediately.

Brazil Nut Brittle

Ingredients

150g (5oz) Brazil nuts, chopped
150g (5oz) dark chocolate
(min 70% cocoa)

SERVES 6

322 calories per serving

Method

Place the chocolate in a bowl and place it over a saucepan of gently simmering water and let it melt. In the meantime, place half of the chopped Brazil nuts in the bottom of a small dish or small loaf tin. When the chocolate has melted and is smooth, pour half of it over the chopped nuts. Add in the remaining chopped nuts and pour over the remaining melted chocolate. Chill in the fridge until it hardens. Break the brittle into chunks and serve.

Apple & Blueberry Ice Lollies

Ingredients

175g (6oz) blueberries
4 apples, peeled, cored and chopped

SERVES
4

69
calories
per
serving

Method

Place all of the ingredients into a blender and process until smooth. Pour the fruit mixture into lolly moulds and place in the freezer until frozen.

Chocolate Orange Cheesecake

Ingredients

800g (1 3/4 lb) cream cheese
4 medium eggs
50g (2oz) 100% cocoa powder
2 teaspoons stevia sweetener powder (or to taste)
5 tablespoons freshly squeezed orange juice

SERVES
10

400
calories
per
serving

Method

Place all of the ingredients into a bowl and combine them. Test the sweetness of the mixture and add extra stevia if necessary. Transfer the mixture to a pie dish and bake at 170C/325F for one hour. Remove the cheesecake and allow it to cool. Serve chilled.

Baked Apples

Ingredients

4 large apples
2 tablespoons raisins
4 teaspoons honey
1/4 teaspoon cinnamon

SERVES 4

145 calories per serving

Method

Core the apples, leaving a small piece at the bottom of the apples to retain the filling. Place the raisins inside the apple and pour a little honey and cinnamon into the centre of each one. Place the apples in the oven and bake at 180C/360F for 35 minutes. Serve with a sprinkling of cinnamon.

109

CONDIMENTS

Kale & Lemon Hummus

Ingredients

200g (7oz) chickpeas (garbanzo beans), drained
2 cloves garlic
25g (1oz) kale leaves, roughly chopped
Juice of 1 lemon, 1 tablespoon olive oil
1 teaspoon sea salt

SERVES 4

97 calories per serving

Method

Place all of the ingredients in a food processor and process until smooth. Serve as a dip or add a spoonful or two to salads.

Watercress Salsa

Ingredients

75g (3oz) fresh watercress
3 tablespoons fresh chopped parsley leaves
1 clove garlic
2 tablespoons olive oil
2 tablespoons lemon juice

SERVES 4

67 calories per serving

Method

Place all the ingredients into a blender and process until smooth. Serve as an accompaniment to meat and fish dishes.

Edamame Dip

Ingredients

275g (10oz) edamame beans (soy beans), fresh or frozen
125g (4oz) plain (unflavoured) yogurt
1 clove garlic, peeled
1 red chilli, de-seeded
1 small onion, peeled and chopped
1 handful of coriander (cilantro), finely chopped
Juice of 1 lime

Method

Cook the edamame beans (soy beans) for 4-5 minutes then rinse them in cold water until cool. Transfer the soya beans to a food processor and add the yogurt, garlic, chilli, onion and lime juice. Process until smooth. Stir in the coriander (cilantro). Serve with crudités.

Olive Tapenade

Ingredients
- 350g (12oz) pitted black olives
- 4 tablespoons fresh parsley
- 1 clove of garlic, peeled
- 25g (1oz) capers
- Juice of ½ lemon
- 2 tablespoons olive oil

SERVES 6

131 calories per serving

Method
Place all the ingredients into a blender and process until slightly chunky.

Lime & Garlic Dressing

Ingredients
- 6 tablespoons olive oil
- 2 tablespoons freshly squeezed lime juice
- 1 clove garlic, crushed
- Freshly ground black pepper

SERVES 6

125 calories per serving

Method
Mix all the ingredients together and store it or use straight away.

Orange & Cumin Dressing

Ingredients

6 tablespoons olive oil
4 tablespoons freshly squeezed orange juice
1 teaspoon paprika
1 teaspoon ground cumin

SERVES 6

127 calories per serving

Method

Combine all the ingredients in bowl and serve with salads. Eat straight away.

Your 7 Day Meal Planner

So many of us have such busy lifestyles that cooking healthy meals from scratch can be overwhelming, so to make life easier this sample meal planner will help you get organised and plan in advance. It shows how you can combine SIRT foods into your meals and stay within your calorie allowance. Just remember 1000 calories for 3 days and 1500 calories for 4 days and you can't go wrong. Always pack in those SIRT foods. Once you get started it'll get easier, plus you'll be finding your favourite meals. You can always make changes to suit your needs. Some people like to make a batch of soup to last several days or to freeze. To keep variety in your diet the sample menu plan has suggestions for different soups but if for handiness you would rather stick to the same soup for consecutive days feel free to make substitutions.

Ideally, pack in those SIRT foods with at least 2 nutritious smoothies a day!

The meal planner shows smoothies as suggestions for breakfast and lunch which is usually more convenient for people who like to have their main meal in the evening but again, switch these around to what suits you best.

	Breakfast	Lunch	Dinner	Snacks	
Day 1 1000 calories	Super SIRT Food Smoothie **173 calories**	Apple & Almond Smoothie **225 calories** Lemon & Rice Soup **84 calories**	Zesty Quinoa Salad **332 calories**	Kale Chips **145 calories**	**TOTAL: 959 calories**
Day 2 1500 calories	Apple & Kale Smoothie **209 calories** Blueberry Compote & Cinnamon Yogurt **178 calories**	Coconut & Chocolate Smoothie **204 calories**	Pork, Kale & Pomegranate **455 calories**	Chocolate Orange Cheese-cake **400 calories**	**TOTAL: 1446 calories**
Day 3 1000 calories	Kale & Papaya Smoothie **160 calories**	Creamy Blueberry Smoothie **188 calories**	Chicken, Kale & Sweet Potato Pie **447 calories**	Fruit & Nut Bar **156 calories**	**TOTAL: 951 calories**
Day 4 1500 calories	Forest Fruits Smoothie **288 calories**	Grape, Avocado & Kale Smoothie **352 calories**	Creole Chicken **416 calories**	Chocolate Mousse **400 calories**	**TOTAL: 1456 calories**

	Breakfast	**Lunch**	**Dinner**	**Snacks**	
Day 5 1000 calories	Super SIRTfood Smoothie **173 calories**	Pomegranate & Blueberry Smoothie **155 calories**	Chicken & Red Wine Casserole **390 calories**	Apple & Walnut Creams **221 calories**	**TOTAL: 939 calories**
Day 6 1500 calories	Creamy Citrus Blend **393 calories**	Clementine & Banana Smoothie **254 calories**	Celeriac & Apple Soup **151 calories** Orange Pork & Leeks **375 calories**	Brazil Nut Brittle **322 calories**	**TOTAL: 1495 calories**
Day 7 1500 calories	Mango & Kale Smoothie **285 calories** Feta & Kale Mini Omelette **113 calories**	Chocolate & Peach Smoothie **196 calories**	Parma Chicken & Capers **314 calories** Balsamic Roast Vegetables **175 calories**	Chocolate Mousse **400 calories**	**TOTAL: 1483 calories**

Made in the USA
Lexington, KY
25 May 2016